Q

is for

Quickie

Magick

Kitchen Table Magick Series

by
G. Alan Joel

Esoteric School of Shamanism & Magic

Email: *alan@shamanschool.com*
Website: *www.shamanschool.com*

Publisher: Esoteric School of Shamanism and Magic, Inc.

Disclaimer and Legal Notice:
The Esoteric School of Shamanism and Magic has made every effort to ensure, at the time of this writing, that the information contained in this book is as accurate as possible. The publisher and author make no warranties or representation with respect to the completeness, fitness, accuracy, applicability, or appropriateness of this book's contents. This book's information is provided strictly for entertainment and educational purposes. Should you choose to use or apply the ideas provided in this book, you take full responsibility for your own actions. The publisher and author provide no guarantee that your life will improve in any way should you choose to use the information presented in this book. The ability of the information provided in this book to provide self-help and life improvement to the reader is entirely dependent upon the reader. The reader's ability to gain positive results from the information presented in this book is entirely dependent on the amount of time the reader devotes to the application of the material in this book, the willingness of the reader to dedicate time and effort to learning the materials presented in this book, as well as the reader's own belief system, which may help or hinder the reader's ability to benefit from this book's materials. Since each reader differs according to willingness and openness to the information available in this book, the author and publisher cannot guarantee success or improvement for every individual reader. Neither the publisher nor the author assumes responsibility for the reader's actions, or whether the information is used for negative or positive purposes. The information contained in this book is drawn from tribal traditions—both modern and ancient—as well as the author's 30 plus years' experience researching and teaching this material to students. The information in this book is presented as interpreted by the author, and, as such, may or may not be entirely accurate. In no way should the information presented in this book be a substitute for advice from health or mental health professionals. The author and publisher are not liable—or in any way responsible—for actions

[this page intentionally left blank]

Quickie Magick Blessing

Child of Wonder,
Child of Flame,
Nourish My Spirit, and
Protect My Aim.

If you need guidance at this moment,
Reach out to the wise owl as your proponent.
With an angel at your service,
No ritual shared shall make you nervous.

In the fast paced world of today,
We understand that time passes quickly away.
So here are quick and simple spells,
Ones that root yourself to mother earth by breathing in her
smells.

Fire energy can be good but can also be too much,
Hug your fridge and let it out through touch.
Knowledge can be learned from the dreams,
Check in with both hands as not everything may be as it
seems.

Pain and tension may cloud your happiness away,
Cool and running water can stop your spirit's fray.
Burn your problems until they are gone,
Use these convenient magick spells until a new dawn.

Thus, my will, so mote it be!

[this page intentionally left blank]

Free Gift

To thank you for purchasing this book, I'd like to give you a

100% FREE GIFT

Learn more about your free magickal gift.

Access Your Free Gift at
www.shamanschool.com

Find a complete list of magickal resources on https://amzn.to/3swxvP0. These resources are constantly updated so check back often!

Kitchen Table Quickie Magick
Table of Contents

[this page intentionally left blank]

Introduction to Kitchen Table Quickie Magick

"We're asking you to trust in the Well-being. In optimism there is magic."
~ Abraham

A Note About This Introduction

This book is one of a series of books in the Kitchen Table Magick series. Each book in the series addresses a specific area of magick (love, money, psychic development, etc.), and is written in a simple "recipe" format for people who want to use magick in their lives immediately. The Kitchen Table Magick series is akin to a Julia Childs recipe book, only these books contain magickal recipes for people to cook up some miraculous and magickal manifestations in their lives.

Because this series was designed so that each person could pick and choose to read just the books that pertain to their current life situation, each book is meant to be readable as a stand-alone book. To introduce the new reader to the series, this introduction to the series is repeated at the beginning of each book. If you have already read one or more books in this series, please feel free to jump ahead to the recipes that interest you. At the same time, some people feel that reviewing the introduction, as well as the "Rules and Tips," is helpful before diving in. In magickal circles, your will is the guideline so choose whichever route best suits you... the Universe and magickal beings will follow!

What is Magick?

Many people have multiple different ideas about what magick is or can be. For the sake of clarity, here is what we know about magick after more than 35 years of study and practice. Magick is a precision science! It is also:

- The science of deliberate creation.
- The science of effective prayer.
- The science of manifesting Higher Will (substitute whatever Higher Force is most familiar to you) on the energetic and material planes.
- The science of heightened awareness, selective perception, and dynamic, harmonious relationships.
- The study of intention (as per Aleister Crowley, one of the greatest magickal practitioners in history).
- The system of creation, not coercion. Note: The word manipulation is often used in conjunction with magick, but manipulation simply means the use of the hands. It should be an "OK" word without a lot of charge, but currently it is used mostly to mean coercion. Look it up!
- The principle that every intentional act is a magickal act! Magick gives us the ability to communicate with beings on all levels, and allows us to understand, through direct experience, the actual workings of the Universe.
- The traditional path of spiritual growth.
- Not extraordinary knowledge. It is the "normal" way of life. We've just lost access to it. When you have this kind of knowledge in your understanding, you have the ability to resolve spiritual questions that otherwise become catechism. From a magickal point of view, catechism is not acceptable, since a practitioner must

experience and verify everything for him or herself. It avoids the trap of dogma. In past times, having a magickal foundation was essential so that we could talk directly to higher beings in the Universal hierarchy.
- Necessary to effective religious practice.

There is some confusion as to how to spell the word "magick." There are three different commonly used spellings: magick, magic, and majick. Eliphas Levi first used the form "magick" to differentiate religious or ceremonial from stage magick. All forms of spelling are acceptable in what this author teaches.

"I love Kitchen Table Magick! It's the best mix of both mystical and down-to-earth magick I have ever encountered. The fact that I can use items from my pantry is so handy and fun! It literally is about cooking up magick at my kitchen table, and having love show up in the least expected places!"
~ Wendy J., Skokie, IL

Is Magick Real?

Yes. Magick is very real and has existed as a precise science for thousands of years. Whether you use the word magick or another name, this spiritual practice is very real. Every single person can learn to do magick. We are ALL born with the talents and abilities that empower us to do magick. The only reason that magick seems so, well, magickal is that this society no longer teaches the art and science of magick. In the distant past, magickal study was just as important as math, science, or the arts. In fact, magick was and still is the birthright of EVERY planetary citizen.

Can you learn to do the kind of magick portrayed in the movies? Yes... and no. The movies are great at giving you a taste of what you can do with magick, but they are not very accurate. In the Harry Potter movies, for instance, the characters use their Wands for every magickal operation. In reality, you can only use the Wand to handle Air energies. Your Wand would actually explode or catch fire if you tried to use it to throw Firebolts and Fireballs as the characters do in the movie.

So, what can you actually do with magick? Quite a lot. Here is a short list to get you started:

- Balance your energies for healing and manifestation
- Change old beliefs
- Defend yourself against physical and psychic attack
- Heal yourself and others
- Find hidden information and see possible futures (and change the future if you do not like the probable futures you divine)
- Psychically communicate with other beings
- Create sacred space
- Find lost people and objects
- Manifest what you want and need in life

At the very basis of magick is the understanding of the four elements: Air, Fire, Water, and Earth. Called elemental magick, these foundational elements are real. Air, Fire, Water, and Earth are part of our natural everyday environment. What makes them magickal is the understanding of how they operate not just on the physical level, but also at the levels of Mind and Spirit.

For instance, while on the physical level, Air is just the stuff we breathe. On the magickal levels Air is the conduit of psychic communication, enlightenment, understanding, dreaming, and more. If you want more of these things in your life, then you need more magickal Air. How do you get more magickal Air? Wear more Air colors, including white for communication and sky blue for enlightenment and understanding. To take this one step further, you could also use various magickal techniques to take on more Air to make your body lighter. Take on enough Air and you'll be able to levitate.

By just extending your understanding and use of the basic ingredients of nature, you are doing magick! Seen in this light, magick isn't all smoke and mirrors, nor is it the result of Hollywood special effects. Magick is the result of truly understanding and working with the very elements that are all around you.

One final note: Many masters, including Wayne Dyer, have said, "You'll see it when you believe it." The same is true for magick. In other words, the suspension of disbelief and the willingness not to exercise contempt prior to investigation are requirements for magick to be "real." Magick is all around us, and always is, but our ability to perceive and use the forces of magick depends on our willingness to be open. No one else can show it to you, only your direct experience and observation can "prove" or demonstrate to you that magick is real.

[this page intentionally left blank]

What is Kitchen Table Magick?

Kitchen Table Magick is exactly what it sounds like—a series of simple recipes that you can literally "cook up" at your kitchen table using household ingredients from your own pantry and cupboard.

The Kitchen Table Magick books have been created for ordinary people who want to mix up a little magick in their lives without all the fancy rituals, but simply with everyday ingredients that can be found in the kitchen pantry, bathroom medicine cabinet, or even stuffed in the back of the junk drawer.

The goal of these books is to allow anyone with the desire to learn this craft to mix up magick literally at the kitchen table using simple recipes. What goes into a simple recipe?

- Everyday items as ingredients
- Easy to follow instructions that don't require years of training
- Procedures that take less than two hours from start to finish
- Built-in expertise that allows the magick to do the heavy lifting
- Some friendly advice on how you can help your magickal recipe provide the best results
- Oh, and a few little rules and guidelines about magickal practice in this specific arena that will keep you safe and sound, magickally speaking, when you use these recipes

Kitchen Table Magick Equals:
Quick – Effective – Safe – Everyday Use – Ordinary
Affordable Ingredients

Why Use Kitchen Table Magick?

- Everyone can do magick.
- Magick should be simple, effective, and start working right away, else it is not magick.
- Not everyone has the time or resources to enroll in a school.
- People ask us for magickal help in hundreds of emails everyday... Kitchen Table Magick is designed to help these very people.
- Of the many areas of life, most people only seem to need help in one or two areas, so you need only buy those Kitchen Table Magick books that apply to your needs.
- Magick is for the masses, and should be accessible, affordable, and simple to do. This is what our teacher taught us, and this is the legacy we are paying forward as well.
- While there are many more advanced forms of magick, these books are an introduction to that world so that you can dabble, experiment, try things out, see the result, adjust and amend, and generally have fun... just as you would cooking a meal in your kitchen.
- This book is not for the major foodie, but it is perfect for the person who needs magickal help right here, right now!

Who Should Use These Recipes?

- You and anyone you know who would like a little more magick and a little less ordinary reality in their lives.
- Anyone who needs help RIGHT now and doesn't have time to fly to India or Sedona to sit at the feet of a guru.

- Anyone who does not have access to anything but a computer for help and guidance.
- Anyone who wants to do magick and then forget it (all while quietly watching the magick "do its thing").
- Anyone who wants affordable, down to earth magick they can do with regular ingredients in the comfort of home.

When to Use Kitchen Table Magick: Anytime...

- You need help.
- You don't want to do all the heavy lifting (leave that to the Angels, Spirit Guides, Animal Totems, and so forth).
- You seem stuck in a rut or corner with no way out.
- You've been struggling with a problem for a long time and need a resolution.
- You don't know what to do but you need to do SOMETHING.
- You'd like to learn how to practice the craft.
- You want to live a more magickal life and stop dealing with ordinary hassles all the time.

How Do We Know These Recipes Work?

- We teach a slew of these recipes in one-day workshops all over the country, via teleconference, and via videoconference. We also email them to people as part of our school's service work, or post them on our blogs and articles library.
- We have used them for over 35 years and still do, every single day – literally tested out at our own kitchen tables for over 35 years (and at thousands of kitchen tables around the world) for a quarter century or more.
- We receive all kinds of stories and testimonials from happy successful students.

Kitchen Table Quickie Magick at Work...

Read the following example to discover how Quickie Magick works in real life...

Going to the Spirit of the Owl for Help

"One of the things that drives me the craziest is when people gossip and plot behind my back. But it seems like any time you put three or more people together, you get that kind of action. What I hated the most is that that kind of behavior could get me in trouble down the road (with the boss, with the spouse, with a committee at work) because it could blindside me.

That's when I learned about the Spirit of Owl. You know how Owls can turn their heads almost 360 degrees, and how they have amazing night vision? It's really hard to hide anything from owls.

Magickally, if I want to learn anything that the is hidden from me, all I have to do is ask Spirit of Owl for help. This proved to be an amazing hidden asset for me one year when my company was looking to hire a recently-vacated management position. It was a great position, with lots of benefits, and there were a lot of people who applied. Many of them called in favors or lobbied the other managers to vote on their behalf. I'm not very good at that sort of thing. I tend to speak my mind and go straight for what I want.

Knowing that I was at a disadvantage, I asked Spirit of Owl to ride on my shoulder and show me what to do every day. At first, I needed Owl to help confirm that the job was within reach. Then I needed Owl to show me the steps, in ways I could easily understand, to take each day to help me land the position.

Well, I didn't get the job. I was bummed. Then I was surprised. My actions had caught the attention of the corporate headhunter hired by the company to fill the management position. That headhunter liked what she saw in me, and recommended me for another position, even better, in another company. I love working there and I've never looked back—and I've never stopped thanking the Spirit of Owl for the help. Oh yes, and I also keep asking Owl for help in my new job. Owl is the most wonderful companion for helping me avoid unseen pitfalls!"

~ Lee R., Fort Morgan, AL

[this page intentionally left blank]

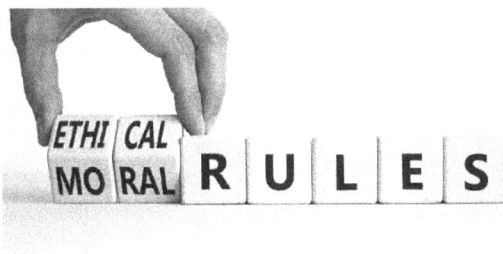

A Few Rules and Tips About Kitchen Table Magick

As with any game, the game of life has its own set of rules. Specifically, the spiritual side of life has rules. Play by those rules and you will stay safe and easily attract what you want into your life. Break those rules and all types of unwanted consequences happen.

These "spiritual rules" are ones that have been observed, both in personal spiritual practice and spiritual practice with various associated groups and teachers. These rules universally govern any spiritual practice and appear to be in effect whether you know them or not. Unlike ethics and morals, which change with culture and time, these spiritual rules appear to have remained the same throughout time, unchanging, like physical and scientific rules.

The rules in the following section are adapted from *Rules of the Road*, as created by George Dew, co-founder of the Church of Seven Arrows. There are two major rules, which are common to most spiritual practices, along with some minor rules that are specific to our form of magickal practice.

Two Major Rules

These two rules will probably sound familiar, as they appear in most major religions and spiritual practices, most probably because they are common-sense and apply not just to spiritual practice, but to life as well.

13

First Rule: Golden Rule or Law of Karma
This first rule is literally a "golden oldie":

What you do to the environment or to other beings in the environment brings similar effects back to you in your life.

Often recognized as the Golden Rule or the Law of Karma, this rule tops the list because it reminds all spiritual practitioners of potential unwanted "rebound" or side effects. As your spiritual power, focus, and abilities grow, this rule will have an ever-greater impact on your life unless you exercise caution. The Universe responds more strongly and powerfully to those with focus, power, and ability.

Note: As humanity moves further in the Aquarian Age, many spiritual practitioners have seen more effects from this rule occur faster. In the past, effects of this rule that often took lifetimes to manifest now occur in minutes, days, weeks, or months. In this particular time in Earth's history, karma seems to operate under a "pay as you go" system. Simply stated, expect the effects of the Law of Karma to occur quickly.

Second Rule: The Judgment of "Good and Bad" According to the Universe
This second rule adds clarity and detail to the first rule described previously:

If you are unsure whether your acts are "good or bad"--that is, whether those acts are in keeping with universal laws on this planet—the Universe will reflect its judgment back to you quickly, according to the "pay as you go" Law of Karma.

This law holds as true for individuals as it does for entire communities, states, nations, or other organized groups. If you are still unsure of the feedback you receive from the Universe, check areas such as your level of health, the soundness of social relationships, your prosperity or lack of, sufficiency of various needs in life, and even your "luck" with appliances and machines. If your luck appears to be consistently poor, then you are probably acting contrary to universal governing laws, regardless of your intentions. The Universe cares about what you do more than what you intend.

Additional Detailed Rules
The following rules offer more detailed standards by which to measure your acts or the acts of others to determine whether these acts are in accordance with universal laws.

- Do nothing that will harm another being unless you are willing to suffer similar or greater harm. What the Universe considers "harm" may be different than what you consider harm.
- Do not bind another being unless you are willing to be similarly bound. An example of binding someone is doing acts in attempt to coerce a specific other person to love you. There is no problem with attracting your soul mate into your life, but doing acts that attempt to coerce a specific other person to love you is a type of binding.
- Never use your spiritual abilities in vain, to show off, or to boost your pride. Using your spiritual abilities from a place of pride usually causes the Universe to bring instant backlash into your life.
- If you choose to charge money or barter for using your spiritual abilities in the service of others, avoid charging extremely high prices. Charge prices for using methods comparable to other professionals, such as an attorney or accountant.
- Never use any spiritual word, chant, litany, or similar "device" unless you are confident in your understanding of its methods, intents, and effects.
- When undertaking a major spiritual operation—one that will require significant effort or attempts to

create a major effect in the world—use divination to determine whether you can safely benefit from such an operation, and to discover the obstacles you must overcome. Divination methods such as pendulum readings, channeling, meditation, and question circles (to name a few) can reveal hidden factors of which you may be unaware.

- In any spiritual endeavor, take your time, think it through, and do it right!

The good news is that you can still use quickie magick rituals. The ones we teach in this book won't get you in trouble with the Universe yet will still allow you to use these quick magickal recipes to make your days a little bit better. The rituals in this book will also help you create space so the Universe can work freely and easily to bring your desired results to you!

The Ingredients of Quickie Magick

"All the most difficult problems become easy when we find the solutions."
~ Debasish Mridha

Life is full of challenges or problems, big and small. Maybe you find yourself stuck in traffic and late for a meeting, or maybe you double-booked yourself and can't figure out how to get out of it, or a thousand other things that can cause you anger, frustration, or upset. Don't worry! We've got some quick fix magickal ritual recipes that work really well for these sort of problems! It may be that you are just "having a bad day" and aren't even sure why. Anytime you need a quick fix in your life, just pull out this recipe book and you'll have simple, totally effective and highly magickal recipes to start using immediately right at your fingertips. The real trick is remembering to use them! We have become so accustomed to simply bearing the conditions in our lives that we often forget we have alternatives. Magicians and shamans always look for solutions rather than staying in the problem. These recipes will hopefully get you started down the path toward a solution whenever you experience a "bump in the road" or something that causes you upset or anger or any other negative or unwanted emotion.

Quickie Magick Appetizer Recipes

Appetizers: In a Hurry? Try These Emergency Helpers

Hire An Angel

Consult with Spirit of Owl for Hidden Information

"I was completely blown away when I heard this: 'Uncounted numbers of angels are unemployed and just waiting for someone to hire them for work. Their rates are reasonable—all they need is some from-the-heart gratitude.' Wow! What an eye opener. And when I figured out that I could hire angels for just about anything, on the spot? I started a full-time employment agency for unemployed angels. My whole tribe benefits, and the pay, gratitude, is such a wonderful price!"
~ Charlie S., Eugene, OR

[this page intentionally left blank]

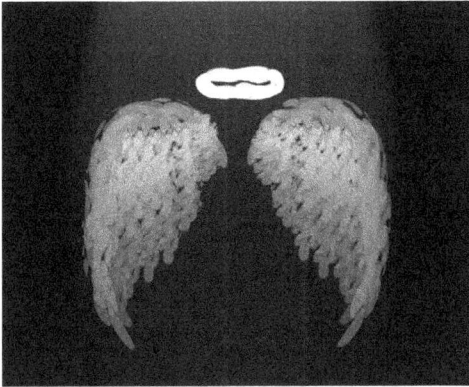

Hire An Angel

"Millions of spiritual creatures walk the earth Unseen,
both when we wake and when we sleep."
~ John Milton, Paradise Lost

Time Required: Fifteen Minutes

Anytime you need a little help to smooth things out or make life a little easier, hire an angel. When you find yourself stuck in traffic, dealing with a sticky situation or just plain late, angels are just waiting to be asked to help you out. Angels are great at quick fixes. They can help you find the best parking space at a busy mall, end a tiresome meeting quickly, help you manifest needed resources or even smooth over a dinner with the in-laws and so much more.

Ingredients
- Belief in higher beings and their willingness to help you.
- Time to properly complete and reflect on the recipe.

Recipe Directions

1. Say out loud or in your mind, "I would like to a request an angel specializing in [traffic, parking places, in-laws, etc.]."

2. Pause for a few moments for the angel to come to you. After you have worked with them for a while you will probably begin to feel a presence. It doesn't take long for them to come to you.

3. Say, "Angel specializing in [your topic], I would like to request your help in [state your case]. Thank you in advance for your help."

4. Once you have received what you have asked for, be sure to thank the angel again. It is VERY IMPORTANT to thank angels so they will be willing to help you later. It's the form of payment you exchange for their help.

How to Use the Results of Your Recipe

There are angels for anything you could possibly need help with, from dealing with particular people to telling you how much salt to put on your food. You can ask their help in absolutely anything. Part of their job is to help us – they can't move on to the next level of their evolution unless they help us, and they can't help us unless we ask for help. Groups of angels are just waiting for us to ask them to help. But don't take them for granted. Really appreciate them. Also know that angels can't go against your will unless you ask for that specifically. For instance, suppose you ask for an angel to help you get a job. If you are repeating negative thoughts in your head over and over about how you can't possibly get a job, the angel can't override that inner vibration you are putting out. However, you can request that one angel help you to stop thinking so negatively about whether you will get a job, and another angel to help you get a job. It is also important to note that lengthy relationships aren't required to work with angels – you can hire one on the spot.

[this page intentionally left blank]

Consult with Spirit of Owl for Hidden Information

"I don't need to know everything.
I just need to know where to find it when I need it."
~ Albert Einstein

Time Required: Fifteen Minutes

If you're not exactly sure why you are having a bad day or just don't have any idea how to get back on track, consulting with the Spirit of Owl can help you gain information and insight. Whether you need information on what others are thinking or planning, insights into your own problems, or help choosing what is the best way for you to go on an issue, Owl is a great partner to work with.

Ingredients
- Willingness and openness to work with higher beings.
- Patience in gaining understanding of messages and

communications from higher beings.

Recipe Directions

1. Either out loud or in your mind say, "Spirit of Owl, I request your help."

2. Pause for a few moments until you feel the presence of Owl (only takes a few seconds).

3. State your request. For instance, if you need help seeing what's causing an illness, you might say, "Owl, please come with me today and show me what is causing this illness in my body. Please show me in a way that I can clearly understand. Thank you in advance for your help." Appreciation is important so don't skip this step.

4. Your answer may come to you now or later throughout the day so stay open to what Owl will show you. Owl may bring up old memories, send you a phrase from the mouth of a stranger or bring a chance meeting with another person. Owl will use any and every device to help you see and clarify the situation you have asked for help with.

5. If at the end of the day, you don't understand what Owl is showing you, ask again the next day. Each day Owl will make it more obvious to you and you will gain a new insight or understanding. You can also specifically ask that information come to you in a way you can easily understand.

6. Be sure each day that you remember to thank Owl for the help.

How to Use the Results of Your Recipe

In many Native American and tribal traditions, Owl is a seer. The Spirit of Owl can assist you in seeing anything that is hidden from you in life. You can ask Owl to help you see anything that you need help with in clarifying a situation such as what's blocking your manifestation, creating an illness, or causing disharmony in your workplace, or wreaking havoc in your relationship with another, or why you are just off balance or grumpy lately. Owl helps you see anything that is hidden from you, including what other people are seeing and feeling.

[this page intentionally left blank]

Quickie Magick Main Course Recipes

Main Courses: All the Help You Need is Within Easy Reach

Root Yourself in Mother Earth

Hug Your Fridge

Check In With Both Hands

"The wisest person I know once told me that I already had all the answers I needed. I laughed and thought that maybe that idea only worked for wise people. Then he taught me this right hand–left hand ritual, in which I ask a question with my dominant hand, and write the answers with my other hand. You know what? The writing is a mess but the answers are golden! We each really do possess all the answers we need within ourselves."
~ Quinn M., Abilene, TX

[this page intentionally left blank]

Root Yourself in Mother Earth

"You carry Mother Earth within you.
She is not outside of you. Mother Earth is not just your
environment."
~ Nhat Hanh

Time Required: Sixty Minutes

On a day where you find yourself in a panic, angry, annoyed, afraid, lacking energy, feeling unbalanced, or just in a bad mood, rooting is a great way to get back on track by grounding and balancing your energies. Rooting allows you to develop "roots" from your palms, heels or base of your spine and plant them into the earth to get rid of unwanted energies and to receive healing energies. Use rooting to balance your energy or mood swings, stay focused in present time and dump negative energy.

Ingredients

- Comfortable place to sit on a chair or on the floor.
- Several minutes of quiet time and space.

Recipe Directions

1. Place your heels, palms or seat (or all three) on the ground. You can extend roots from more than one body part at once.

2. Envision yourself forming roots from your palms, heels or the base of your spine and begin extending those roots with your intention. You don't need to think about it, just do it! Some people find it easier to do with eyes closed.

3. Push your roots through the carpet or tile, into the sub floor and down into the earth. If you are in a multi-level building, you will need to go through each level until you reach the earth. If you are wearing shoes with thick soles, you may have to extend the roots out the sides of your shoes.

4. Once your roots reach the earth keep extending them down through the topsoil and deeper layers until you reach bedrock.

5. When you reach bedrock, lock your roots in.

6. Sit quietly with your roots in the earth and just breathe naturally.

7. With each exhaling breath send any unwanted energies down your roots into the bedrock. The earth is highly receptive and will receive these energies easily.

8. With each inhaling breathe pull in minerals, fluids and other energies from the earth for nourishment

and balancing. You don't have to specify what you're pulling up – your body and your roots will work automatically with the earth to pull up what is needed.

9. Once you feel relaxed and nourished pull your roots back up into your body. Stay seated until you totally pull your "roots" back in.

How to Use the Results of Your Recipe

Always be sure to pull your roots back – if you stand up without doing so you may feel a slight "popping" sensation and your body will be sore for a few days. Rooting can help you feel refreshed, awake, alive and balanced. This quick fix recipe only takes a few minutes and is worth every second! You can use this recipe when you are alone or in public and no one will know what you are doing.

[this page intentionally left blank]

Hug Your Fridge

"To let go is to release the images and emotions, the grudges and fears, the clingings and disappointments of the past that bind our spirit.
~ Jack Kornfield

Time Required: Fifteen Minutes

This recipe can help you out when you find yourself with excess fire energies manifesting as conditions such as pain, stress, anger, inflammation, fever, headache or anxiety. Your refrigerator is an electrical ground or conduit that can be used to ground out your excess fire energy.

Ingredients
- A refrigerator or other large electrically grounded appliance.
- Sun Yellow candle.
- Wooden or paper matches.

Recipe Directions

1. Stand in front of your refrigerator or lie on the floor in front of it.

2. If possible, place the area of pain, stress or inflammation directly on the refrigerator. For instance, if you have a headache in the front of your head, put your forehead on the refrigerator. If you have a headache in the back, put the back of your head on the refrigerator. For general pain or stress all over the body, put your hands on the refrigerator or lie down and put your feet on the refrigerator.

3. Feel yourself pushing and flowing all the energy that you don't want, such as pain or anxiety, into the refrigerator. Fire energy flows quickly, so you won't need to flow for more than a minute or two.

4. After you have flowed out all the excess fire energy, if you feel you need an energy boost, light and charge a Sun Candle to replace energy you flowed out with nurturing Sun Yellow energy. A Sun Candle is a pillar candle that is bright yellow with no orange or red tones to it. To charge it, light the candle with paper or wooden matches, cup your hands around and over the flame and say in a voice of command: "Child of Wonder, Child of Flame, Nourish My Spirit and Protect My Aim". Keep the candle lit in the room you are in until you feel re-energized.

How to Use the Results of Your Recipe

You can also use electrical outlets, light switch plates and large electrical appliances, such as an electric stove to ground out excess fire energy. Do NOT ground fire energy into computers, small electrical appliances, lamps or electronics as they can't handle that amount of fire energy and will short out. This is a great recipe to use anytime you find yourself stressed out or with a headache or other physical pain. You can use it even if you are outside by finding an electrical ground of some type such as a telephone pole.

[this page intentionally left blank]

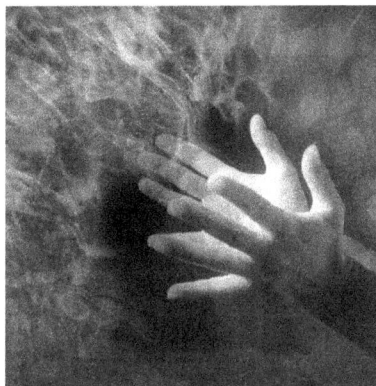

Check In With Both Hands

"You can't reach for anything new if your hands are still full of yesterday's junk"
~Louise Smith

Time Required: Sixty Minutes

Your daily life can become much more enjoyable the more you ask for help and information from angels, guides, animal totems or your own Spirit. Mind tends to tell us things that have been tainted by society or that stem from misperceptions, but Spirit always gives us truth and doesn't lead us astray. Often a bad day is simply the result of these misperceptions from Mind and this recipe, for the Left Hand, Right Hand Ritual can help you get a grip on the day by making you a channel for the information you need or want to access. Basically you ask yourself questions with your dominant hand and answer them with your other hand.

Ingredients

- The ability to be patient with the process (the process can be a bit "hit or miss" in the beginning)
- The willingness to keep practicing the ritual until you get the desired result
- Quiet time before bed to set your intention for directed dreaming
- Your dream diary to chart your progress and record results

Recipe Directions

1. Use your compass to find the cardinal direction East. This recipe requires you to sit in the East facing West, so it is important to make sure you have the correct direction identified. East is the direction of knowledge and communication therefore sitting in the East will facilitate this communication ritual and help you access knowledge.

2. Sit in the East facing West with a table in front of you.

3. Place your Sun Yellow candle, wooden or paper matches, and a pen and paper on the table.

4. Light the candle and charge it. To charge the Sun Candle, refer to the "Hug Your Fridge" recipe for the procedure.

5. Write your question or questions that you are seeking information about on the paper using your dominant hand (the hand you naturally point with) to hold the pen. For example, you may have just gone through a traumatic event and you might write, "What lesson am I to learn from (describe your current event or situation)?

6. Now switch the pen to your other hand and write the answer without stopping to think. Just write the first

thing that your hand feels inspired to write. It doesn't matter what the writing looks like as long as it is legible to you so don't spend time worrying about that.

7. Sometimes you may be surprised at the answer or the answer may not make sense to you. Don't try to force sense from it. Keep the answer in your consciousness for a few days and see what happens. It may be that you have only received a partial answer so that it will be easier to digest and other things will come up to fill in blanks. Be sure to blow out the candle when you are finished writing.

How to Use the Results of Your Recipe

You can repeat this recipe as many days as you need to until you get all the information you need. Be patient with the process and enjoy watching the knowledge and understanding unfold as the results become clearer. Your answers will come in perfect timing with your ability to process and use them.

[this page intentionally left blank]

Quickie Magick Dessert Recipes

Desserts: Quickie Magick for Hot or Cold

Shower and Bathtub Litany

The Big Burn

"Catharsis is a major way to clear blockages in life, be they emotional, mental, relationship, or any other type of hang-up. I fully admit I am an adrenaline junkie so when I read about the cold magick of the shower litany versus the hot magick of the big burn... I was all about the big burn. It's cathartic. All I have to do is write down my problems, which gets them out of me and onto a piece of paper, and then use the right magickal tools to burn 'em up! I love the big burn and I use it all the time!"
~ Benjamin E., Santa Fe, NM

[this page intentionally left blank]

Shower and Bathtub Litany

"Let the rain wash away, all the pain of yesterday"
~ Skylar Grey

Time Required: Fifteen Minutes

Have you had a chaotic, crazy, hectic day? If so, then here's a recipe for you! You can literally wash tension, strain and pain off your body in the shower or bathtub using the shower litany.

Ingredients
- Access to a shower or other type of cool running water that you can stand under.
- Or a tub of cool water that you can drain the water out of.

Recipe Directions
1. Run water in your shower until the water temperature is cool (just below body temperature). Too cold

creates tension and too hot won't carry fire energy away.

2. Get in the shower with your back to the showerhead.

3. Move the showerhead so that the water is hitting you at the base of the skull and the water is able to run evenly over your back and front.

4. Stand this way in the stream of water and feel the tension or pain or other fire type energy moving down your body being absorbed by the water.

5. If you need to you can run your hands down your body to bring the tension and pain down to your feet.

6. Picture and "feel" the tension and pain mixing with the water and flowing down the drain, while simultaneously repeating the following litany aloud in a voice with authority and power.

"All the tension, all the strain,
All the pain with excess flame,
Flow with water, down the drain!"

7. Keep saying the litany until you feel all the tension and pain leave your body.

How to Use the Results of Your Recipe

The shower litany will wash away any inflammation, pain, headache, tension or stress that you have accumulated during the day. Using it daily will help you avoid picking up fire energies such as stress, pain and anxiety throughout your day. Used daily, it can also help you feel more balanced and more energetic. Use reminders with laminated sticky notes that have the verse printed on them in your bathroom or in the shower so you don't forget to use this recipe as a daily ritual. You can also do this ritual in a bathtub filled with cool water by seeing the fire energies flowing out of your body, being absorbed by the water and then draining the water from the tub and watching them flow down the drain. Say the litany in the same way as for the shower litany, remaining in the tub until all the water drains out taking the fire energies with it.

[this page intentionally left blank]

The Big Burn

"Holding on to anger is like grasping a hot coal with the intent of throwing it at someone else; you are the one who gets burned."
~ Buddha

Time Required: Thirty Minutes

The Big Burn ritual is great for literally "burning away" anything unwanted, including negativity, fear, and other factors in life that are no longer useful. It is especially good for burning off anger. When you find yourself overwhelmed with anger or other negative feelings or situations, just get out your Firebowl, this recipe, and do the Big Burn. Magickally melt those problems away so you can enjoy life.

Ingredients

- Magickal firebowl (see #1 in directions)
- Ground fire clay or clean, fine sand.
- Self-starting charcoal.
- Wooden or paper matches.
- Finely chopped or shaved wood chips.
- Pine resin.
- Finely ground or rubbed sage.
- Sun Candle.
- Pen and plenty of blank paper.

Recipe Directions

1. When choosing a Firebowl, look for one that is made of brass, cast-iron, ceramic or a hard hardwood. It should be 4-6 inches in diameter and 4-5 inches deep. It should also be a shape that is easily held with one or both hands and light enough to carry in one hand if necessary. Make sure your Firebowl is of a shape that will be stable when placed on a flat surface. The shape of the bowl should also be curved-in and flared back out at the top rim to promote "columning" of incense or smoke. Fill it with ground fire clay or clean, fine sand. Non-scented cat litter (which is ground clay) works well as long as it does not have chemicals or deodorants in it. Put 1-2 inches in the bottom of your Firebowl as an insulator to protect the Firebowl itself, your hands and any surfaces from the heat.

2. Charge your Firebowl by following these steps:
   - Light your Sun Yellow candle with a wooden or paper match.
   - Light another wooden or paper match from your candle flame and use this to light a charcoal disk. The disk will begin to spark within seconds. If the charcoal is old or damp, you may need to use metal tongs to hold it over the flame for several minutes or light the top of it in the center of the

bowl-shaped depression. Most of you will realize that once the disk is lit, you don't touch it with your hands, but for beginners who have never used one before we like to add this word of caution – It is hot, just like a charcoal on a BBQ grill.

- Once the charcoal sitting in your Firebowl is lit, pull Sun Yellow energy from your candle into yourself and blow it out onto the disk.
- Add wood shavings onto the charcoal, then the pine resin and finally the sage.
- Wait for it to produce a good column of smoke and add more sage or resin if needed.
- A voice of command should be used when programming the Firebowl for the Big Burn ritual by saying the charge verse:

"Fire and Air where you are cast,
Let no spell nor adverse purpose last,
Not in accord with me!
Clear from my life these unwanted matters,
Send far from my life these negative factors!
Thus my will, so it be!"

3. Now sit in the South facing North with your lit Sun Candle, charged Firebowl and pen/paper in front of you.

4. Start writing everything that is bothering you or making you feel negative on your blank pieces of paper. Keep writing as fast as you can and get everything out on the paper. Write as much as you need to and don't worry if you repeat yourself. Write until you literally run out of steam (combination of Fire and Water energy).

5. Now you are ready for the Big Burn part of the ritual. Place your Firebowl in front of you (be sure your Firebowl is large enough to accommodate the burning of the papers – if not, move the entire operation to the

sink or some other place that is safe for burning or move outside to a fire ring if you will be burning enough to create a lot of smoke or that is not safe to burn inside).

6. Take a moment to do whatever you need to do to move the anger or negative feelings out of yourself. You might ask for help from angels, ask for guidance, just have a moment of silence, or take several deep breaths.

7. Now, light the papers with your wooden or paper match and let it burn in the Firebowl. You can light each sheet individually (many people find this method more satisfying), or wad up the whole mess of papers and light the entire thing (again observing fire safety precautions).

8. Then sit back and watch your anger go up in smoke.

How to Use the Results of Your Recipe

If you are dealing with a chronic or stubborn problem, you may need to do the Big Burn on a daily basis for 40 days or more. This will give you 40 days of making a daily conscious contact with the Universe. Doing this technique as a daily ritual will also build the strength of your spell matrix for 40 days in a row. While some experts feel that bad habits or chronic conditions can be handled in less than 40 days, spiritually the number 40 is very effective.

More Magickal Resources

Kindle or Paperback on Amazon:

1. ***Witchcraft Spell Book Series:***
   - Learn How to Do Witchcraft Rituals and Spells with Your Bare Hands (Witchcraft Spell Books, Book 1)
   - Learn How to Do Witchcraft Rituals and Spells with Household Ingredients (Witchcraft Spell Books, Book 2)
   - Learn How to Do Witchcraft Rituals and Spells with Magical Tools (Witchcraft Spell Books, Book 3)
   - Witchcraft Spell Book: The Complete Guide of Witchcraft Rituals & Spells for Beginners (compilation of Books 1, 2 & 3)
2. ***Kitchen Table Magick Series***

Ebooks and Online Courses at *www.shamanschool.com*

- Wand: Air Tool
- Athame: Fire Tool
- Chalice: Water Tool
- Plate: Earth Tool
- Magical Tool: Firebowl
- Psychic Development
- Energy Healing For Self and Others

- How to Do Voodoo
- Daily Rituals to Attract What You Want in Life

Find a complete list of magickal resources on https://amzn.to/3swxvPo. These resources are constantly updated so check back often!

Free Gift Offer

To thank you for purchasing this book, I'd like to give you a

100% FREE GIFT

Learn more about your free magickal gift.

Access Your Free Gift at www.shamanschool.com

Find a complete list of magickal resources on https://amzn.to/3swxvPo. These resources are constantly updated so check back often!

About G. Alan Joel

Magick means many things to different people. The form of magick taught by G. Alan Joel for more than 30 years is steeped in tribal traditions from around the world, from both modern tribal cultures and those from the past, which have been mostly passed on through oral dialog.

At the very heart of the magick that Mr. Joel teaches is the use of Universal Laws for the benefit of self, others, and even the planet. These magickal traditions can take on many forms, including simple rituals for daily use, specific spells for particular life situations, the use of simulacra (often better known as voodoo), weather working, water witching, the use of the elemental tools (Firebowl, Wand, Athame, Chalice, and Plate), magickal self-defense rituals, and more. Also included are the use of the Tarot for divination and spellwork, divination rituals of all kinds, Spirit-to-Spirit communication, exercises for psychic development, and abundant healing techniques.

Through his 30 plus years of studying, teaching, and honing his magickal practice, G. Alan Joel has helped thousands of people successfully integrate the magickal, and seemingly miraculous, into their daily lives. In fact, one of the greatest gifts Mr. Joel has offered through his teachings is the ability for his students to always find a magickal solution for life situations that often seem impossible to solve. With magick, anything is possible in the mundane world. All that is required of the practitioner is an open mind, the desire to learn, and a willingness to pay some time and effort into his or her magickal practice. One of Mr. Joel's favorite quotes is:

"What you pay into your practice pays you back!"

While many magickal traditions have fiercely guarded their secrets from the public, Mr. Joel feels that "Magick is the birthright of every planetary citizen." As such he strives to offer magickal teachings that are easily learned and inexpensive (no excessive fees to join exclusive magickal groups or ascend up the levels of learning). He also offers techniques that are usable and effective for all who are sincere in their desire to practice magick. In essence, Mr. Joel's methods teach a form of "Every Man's (and Woman's) Magick." All are welcome, his teachings are simple yet effective, and he also offers online classes in which he helps students troubleshoot their magickal issues in an interactive setting.

Find out more about Mr. Joel's teachings here and on his website (***www.shamanschool.com***) where magickal offerings are updated on a regular basis.

Mr. Joel augments this magickal knowledge and teaching with 30 years of practice as Doctor of Chinese Medicine, including a deep understanding of herbology and acupuncture. His understanding of the healing arts deepens the magickal knowledge he teaches, as magickal healing is a major aspect of his teachings. Mr. Joel believes that while there is clearly a time and place for Western Medicine, magickal and Eastern healing techniques can be harmoniously blended in to offer people many choices for healing all types of health conditions.

About the Esoteric School of Shamanism and Magic

The Esoteric School of Shamanism and Magic was started from a desire for all people from all over the globe to be able to attend a real, if virtual, school dedicated to magick and shamanism. The aim of the Esoteric School of Shamanism and Magic is to help people create permanent, positive change in their lives through the study of esoteric magickal and shamanic knowledge. It doesn't matter what your esoteric background is, whether you started out with witchcraft, religious studies, spirituality, or candle magick, we welcome you. We believe that the Truth is the same, no matter which form you practice. We delight in all manner of shamanic schools and traditions, magickal techniques and esoteric ritual. You can visit us at ***www.shamanschool.com***, our blog at ***http://shamanmagic.blogspot.com***, or on social media via links on our website.

[this page intentionally left blank]

[this page intentionally left blank]

[this page intentionally left blank]

[this page intentionally left blank]

www.ingramcontent.com/pod-product-compliance
Lightning Source LLC
Chambersburg PA
CBHW071930020426
42331CB00010B/2800